Jaime Escalante

A Man Who Made a Difference

Darleen Ramos

Contents

Rigby
A Harcourt Achieve Imprint

www.Rigby.com
1-800-531-5015

1 Life in Bolivia

If you were asked to name your hero, you might choose a professional athlete, or maybe a music star. But would you ever choose a teacher? Some of the students who attended Garfield High School in California between 1976 and 1991 would name Jaime Escalante as their hero. He was a teacher who motivated them to succeed when they believed success was impossible. He inspired in them the desire to always do their best and the ability to achieve their goals.

Early Years

Jaime Escalante was born on December 31, 1930, in La Paz, Bolivia. His parents, Zenobio and Sara Escalante, were schoolteachers who were assigned by the government to teach in a small Aymara Indian village in the *altiplano*, or the high plateau area of Bolivia. There, tucked in the Andes Mountains, Jaime spent his days making up games. On sunny afternoons, he would visit the plaza and play word games or solve puzzles with his grandfather, who was a retired teacher.

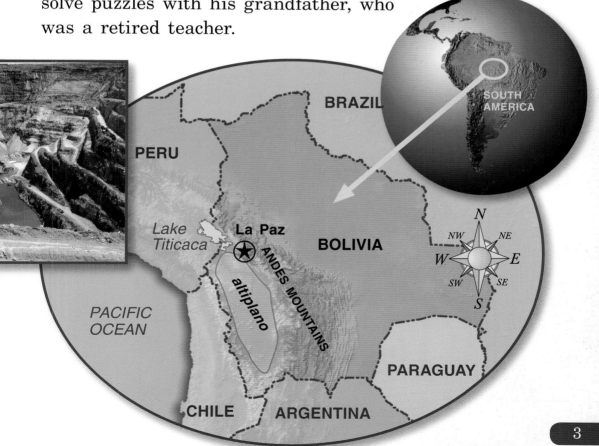

School Days

Jaime's parents eventually separated, and his mother moved Jaime and his siblings to La Paz, Bolivia's capital. Jaime started elementary school, and it was obvious to everyone that he was very good at math and science. In his spare time, he built wooden carts to coast down the hilly streets, performed his own experiments with electricity, and played handball. Jaime's mother knew he was a brilliant student and that his **education** was important, so she saved enough money to send him to a private high school, San Calixto.

Jaime loved his new school, and his love for solving puzzles proved helpful in his quest to solve math problems. Rather than working on problems with the class, Jaime would work ahead and finish his math book long before his classmates. But Jaime had a playful side, too, and it often got him into trouble. He was known for teasing his teachers, and he often amused his classmates with his jokes.

La Paz, the capital of Bolivia, rests in a canyon of the *altiplano*. From the city you can see the tall peaks of the Andes Mountains.

2 Growing Up

When Jaime graduated from San Calixto, he wanted to go to engineering school, but, unfortunately, his dream would have to wait. Jaime's mother had little money to support the family, so Jaime worked in order to help her. However, Jaime's attention soon turned to the instability and unrest in his country.

Bolivia was like a battlefield, for the country had been politically unstable for many years. Many Bolivian presidents who were elected were quickly overthrown by people with different beliefs. War and revolution were a way of life.

Palacio Quemado, the presidential palace of Bolivia

In the 1940s most Bolivian people were either extremely poor or extremely wealthy. New political parties claimed that they could make changes. In 1949 one of these political parties started uprisings in towns around La Paz, and Jaime, then 19 years old, decided to join the army in the short-lived revolution. After the government quickly put an end to the uprising, Jaime and other new volunteers were sent away. He was home within days, jobless and broke.

Life in Bolivia is still not easy, as more than half of the people live in poverty.

Starting a Teaching Career

A friend suggested to Jaime that the two of them attend a teacher training college and become teachers. They both passed their entrance exams and became college students. During his second year in college, Jaime was asked to teach a class at a high school. One of Jaime's former elementary school teachers had recommended him. He had thought that Jaime would be perfect for the job. Although Jaime was not a licensed teacher, he accepted the job, for he needed to earn some money.

How is this Bolivian classroom similar to or different from your classroom?

Jaime was inexperienced and had no idea how to teach, but he was committed to helping his students learn. In Bolivia, one teacher gives the final exam to another teacher's students. Jaime's stomach was a bundle of nerves because his students' performance was a reflection of his teaching. To his delight they passed their final exam!

While still attending college, Jaime received two more job offers—one at the National Bolivar High School and the other at San Calixto High School, the school where he had once studied and teased his teachers. Jaime accepted both offers.

A Tough Teacher

Bolivia was in need of educators and Jaime was gaining recognition as a good teacher. Even though he did not yet have his teaching license, he was now working at three schools! Jaime was a challenging teacher, and he expected his students to always do their best. He gave a lot of homework and tough tests. When he heard about an engineering school holding a contest, he enrolled his best students from San Calixto. They lost the first year, but Jaime did not allow himself or his students to become discouraged.

In 1954 Jaime married Fabiola Tapia, a young woman he had met who was also seeking her teaching degree. A year later their son Jaime, Jr. was born. Life was good for the new Escalante family, and they seemed happy.

In 1961, however, the government in Bolivia was still unstable. Although the Escalantes were doing well, Fabiola wanted to leave Bolivia and move to the United States, but Jaime wanted to stay.

3 Moving to the United States

During 1961 Jaime attended a program to study arts and science in Puerto Rico, which also gave him the opportunity to tour the United States. He saw the White House, met President John F. Kennedy, and visited Niagara Falls, but Jaime was most inspired by a high school he saw in Tennessee. It was a wonderful place with large halls, basketball courts, and an amazing science laboratory! It was then that Jaime decided that he wanted to teach in an American high school.

Jaime attended the Alliance for Progress program, which was created by U.S. President John F. Kennedy.

Immigrants to the United States must prepare special papers before they enter the country.

Fabiola prepared the **immigration** papers to get permission to live in the United States and asked her brother to be their **sponsor**. Jaime would go to the United States first and find a job and a house, and Fabiola and Jaime, Jr. would come later.

In 1963 Jaime was one of hundreds of immigrants from Bolivia who came to the Los Angeles area to start a new life. At the age of 33, Jaime arrived in the United States, hoping to teach in an American school, but once again his dream would have to wait. First he had to learn how to speak English.

Sponsorship for Immigration

The Escalantes needed a sponsor to enter the United States. A sponsor is someone who is willing to financially support an immigrant until he or she becomes a U.S. citizen. Samuel, Fabiola's brother, was living in Los Angeles, and he agreed to sponsor the Escalante family.

Life in Los Angeles

Jaime found a job mopping floors at a restaurant. In Bolivia teachers are highly respected, and Fabiola's brother, Samuel, thought Jaime should remember that his goal was to teach in the United States. Samuel took Jaime to enroll at Pasadena City College to learn English and other skills. Jaime had to take an entrance test, and he chose the math test because math is the same in every language. Within just 25 minutes, he completed the two-hour test with a perfect score!

When Jaime and his family came to the United States, they settled in the busy city of Los Angeles, California.

The next year Fabiola and Jaime, Jr. moved to California. Fabiola was upset that Jaime was not teaching, yet he was making more money working in the restaurant than he had when he taught in Bolivia.

But Jaime was anxious to start teaching again. When he felt he knew enough English, he wrote to the California Department of Education, hoping to get a teaching license. Their reply was not encouraging, for California would not accept his teaching degree from Bolivia. Jaime would have to complete a teaching program in the United States.

Starting Over

Jaime was terribly upset by this news. He would have to start all over, working at night and going to school during the day, which could take years. If he wanted to, Jaime could move back to Bolivia. However, the educational opportunities for Jaime, Jr. in the United States were better than those in Bolivia, so Jaime continued to go to school and work. He was promoted to be the cook at the restaurant and later got a job at an electronics factory.

Jaime had an important decision to make, and he carefully considered all of his options.

	Bolivia	United States
Family	His mother and siblings were living in Bolivia.	Fabiola and Jaime, Jr. liked living in Los Angeles.
Career	Jaime could go back to teaching immediately.	Jaime would have to work while he went to college.
Education	Opportunities were not as good as in the United States.	Opportunities were better than in Bolivia.
Finances	Jaime would earn less money.	Jaime would earn more money.

California State University

Although the work at the electronics factory was more challenging for Jaime than the work at the restaurant, solving electrical problems reminded Jaime of teaching. Then Jaime learned about a scholarship that might help him get his teaching degree more quickly. After ten years of learning English, taking night classes, and working for minimum wage, Jaime graduated from California State University in 1974. Jaime, now a U.S. citizen, was offered a teaching job at Garfield High School in East Los Angeles. His dream was becoming a reality!

4 Building a Math Program

East Los Angeles is a community where many Hispanic immigrants live. Many students at Garfield High School had parents who had immigrated to the United States from Mexico and Latin America. Jaime welcomed the assignment to work at Garfield and was overjoyed to hear that he was going to teach a computer class. But when he arrived to teach in September, he was told he would be teaching basic math classes instead of the computer classes.

Immigrants who come to a new country can often find communities where other people from their home country live.

Jaime wondered why high school students had to take basic math. In addition, the students were disrespectful. Wondering if he had made the right decision, Jaime seriously considered returning to his old job at the electronics factory. But he decided to stay at the high school for one semester.

First Jaime wanted to make the classroom more welcoming, so he invited his students to help paint the walls, clean the desks, and hang posters. Next he demanded that his students be on time for class. And most importantly, he made them work.

Making a Difference

During the summer Jaime worked two jobs at electronics companies. During his second year at Garfield, he asked if he could teach a few algebra classes. The hope of teaching algebra gave him a reason to stay, yet his students still were not motivated to succeed. He did everything he could to inspire them. He even dressed up as a cook, brought in apples, and divided them into halves, quarters, and fifths, hoping to teach his students about fractions.

How can a sliced apple teach students about fractions?

It took several years before Jaime earned a reputation at Garfield as a teacher who expected 100 percent from his students. His students had quizzes, plenty of homework, and no time for mischief. This approach finally motivated his students to learn and solve problems and to succeed in Jaime's class. Jaime's students started to appreciate the value of math and the importance of success as much as Jaime did.

5 A Tough Test

In the fall of 1978, 14 of Jaime's students showed an interest in taking calculus, an advanced type of math used to solve scientific and engineering problems. These students would be able to take an advanced placement calculus test—a test whose results would give them credit toward a college degree.

By the spring, only five students remained in the class to take the test. Jaime was determined to make this program succeed. He had pushed his students in Bolivia, and he would push his students in Los Angeles.

Each year after that, more students signed up for Jaime's class, and each year more students passed the test. During the school year, Jaime's students arrived at school at 7:00 A.M., worked through lunch to study with their teacher, and stayed until 5:00 P.M. to practice more problems. Jaime expected his students to make his class their most important task.

Disappointment and Determination

On the day of the exam in 1982, 18 of Jaime's students arrived to take the test. The first part of the test was multiple-choice, and Jaime's students agreed that this section was very easy. The next part of the test was more difficult because the students had to complete word problems and show their work.

When the tests were graded, the graders noticed that six students had similar calculating errors on one particular problem. The graders wondered if the students had cheated.

Without directly stating so, the testing board suggested that the students had cheated and requested that all 18 students take the test again. Upset and discouraged, the students and Jaime tried to resolve the matter. There was talk about **discrimination** against Hispanic students. By the time the testing board reached its decision, some of the students had already enrolled in college or had moved away. Taking the test after a summer without any studying would be difficult, and the students wondered if they were ready. After much consideration 12 students decided to retake the test, and all 12 passed.

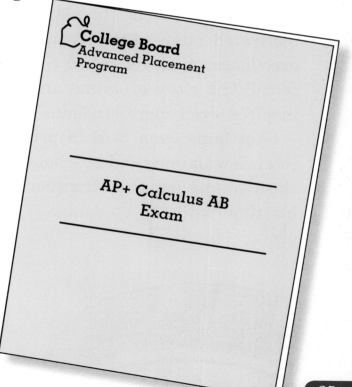

College Board
Advanced Placement
Program

AP+ Calculus AB
Exam

6 A Name to Remember

The story of Jaime Escalante and his **minority** students who took the advanced placement calculus test twice and passed both times made national headlines. Even Jaime's sister in Bolivia heard the story on the radio. She was proud that her brother had gone to the United States and had made a difference. But the news and fame that Jaime received brought changes that were both positive and negative.

The news about the Garfield High School students motivated many other Hispanic students to strive for excellence. A movie called *Stand and Deliver* was made to tell the story of Jaime and his students, and this inspired even more students and teachers.

Yet fame came with a price. Reporters wanted to interview Jaime, and teachers wanted to observe his class. Jaime felt the attention was taking away from his time with the students.

People all over the world heard the news about Jaime and his students. Thousands of miles away, his sister heard the story on the radio. Others learned of this success story when a movie was made based on Jaime's experiences.

Moving On

For the next several years, the calculus program grew, and soon there was so much student interest that there were not enough teachers. Jaime had very large classes, and as a result, test scores were not as good. He continued to ask for more money and teachers, but not everyone at Garfield believed that calculus classes were so important.

In May of 1988, Vice President George Bush visited Jaime's class and answered questions from his students.

In 1991 Jaime left Garfield High School and started teaching math at Hiram Johnson High School in Sacramento, California. Before Jaime arrived at Hiram, six students took the advanced calculus test and all passed. Three years later 18 students passed the difficult test.

In 1997 Jaime decided to retire from teaching at the age of 67. He eventually went back to Bolivia, where he teaches at a university, and he frequently returns to the United States to visit his children.

7 Accomplishments and Awards

After he left teaching, Jaime received many awards and was inducted into the National Teachers Hall of Fame. Jaime Escalante, an immigrant teacher from Bolivia, probably never imagined he would receive such an honor.

Jaime Escalante always believed in hard work. He learned English and committed ten years of his life to going back to school just so he could teach in the United States. Throughout his career as a teacher, both in Bolivia and in the United States, he was dedicated to teaching and expected the same commitment from his students. He believed all students could achieve great things if they were determined, worked hard, and had the desire to succeed.

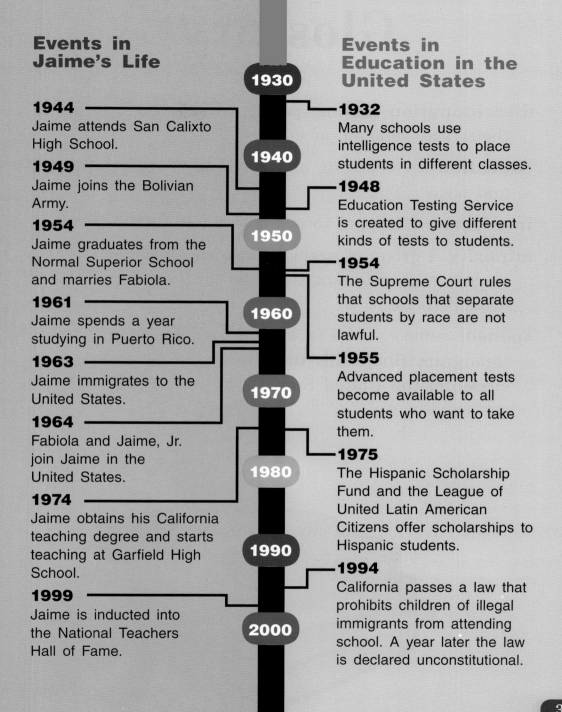

Events in Jaime's Life

1944
Jaime attends San Calixto High School.

1949
Jaime joins the Bolivian Army.

1954
Jaime graduates from the Normal Superior School and marries Fabiola.

1961
Jaime spends a year studying in Puerto Rico.

1963
Jaime immigrates to the United States.

1964
Fabiola and Jaime, Jr. join Jaime in the United States.

1974
Jaime obtains his California teaching degree and starts teaching at Garfield High School.

1999
Jaime is inducted into the National Teachers Hall of Fame.

1930
1940
1950
1960
1970
1980
1990
2000

Events in Education in the United States

1932
Many schools use intelligence tests to place students in different classes.

1948
Education Testing Service is created to give different kinds of tests to students.

1954
The Supreme Court rules that schools that separate students by race are not lawful.

1955
Advanced placement tests become available to all students who want to take them.

1975
The Hispanic Scholarship Fund and the League of United Latin American Citizens offer scholarships to Hispanic students.

1994
California passes a law that prohibits children of illegal immigrants from attending school. A year later the law is declared unconstitutional.

Glossary

discrimination treating people unfairly because of their race, religion, or culture

education the teaching and learning of information and ideas

immigration moving to a new country to live

minority a group of people whose race, religion, or culture is different than the larger group around them

sponsor someone who is willing to support an immigrant financially until he or she becomes a citizen of the United States